Celebrations

CHRISTMAS

Hilary Lee-Corbin

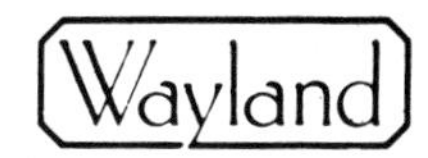

Celebrations

Christmas
Easter
Hallowe'en
Harvest
New Year
Hindu Festivals
Jewish Festivals
Muslim Festivals

All words that appear in **bold** are explained in the glossary on page 46

First published in 1989 by
Wayland (Publishers) Limited
61 Western Road, Hove
East Sussex BN3 1JD, England

British Library Cataloguing in Publication Data
Lee-Corbin, Hilary
Christmas – (Celebrations)
1. Christmas – For Children
I. Title II. Series
394.2'68282

ISBN 1 85210 739 1

Phototypeset by Kalligraphics Ltd, Horley, Surrey

Printed and bound in Italy by G.Canale & C.S.p.A.,Turin

Contents

The Christmas spirit

Christmas celebrates the birth of Jesus, so it is a very important time in the Christian religion.

Christmas is also the best known festival of the year. All over the world, people wish each other a 'Merry Christmas'. Everyone enjoys getting presents from Father Christmas.

At Christmas time, people have fun. They enjoy eating well and having a holiday. But was Christmas always like this? How did it begin?

Many big cities are decorated with beautiful lights at Christmas time.

The story of Christmas

The birthday of Jesus

Jesus' mother Mary lived in Judaea, in the Roman Empire. The Romans told her to go to Bethlehem, but the town was full, so she and Joseph had to stay in a stable. That is where Jesus was born, among the animals in the stable. Wise men and shepherds came to visit the new-born baby.

This painting shows Mary, Joseph and the baby Jesus. ➧

Christmas Day is 25 December. But nobody knows if that was really Jesus' birthday.

Jesus' birthday is often shown in pictures made of coloured glass in church windows.

The Roman Saturnalia

In the northern half of the world, December is the time when the days are very short and dark. At the end of December the sun starts to climb higher. Spring is on its way. The Romans called this the birthday of the sun and had a big festival. It was called **Saturnalia,** after Saturn the god of farming.

Everyone enjoyed themselves at the Roman Saturnalia.

Saturnalia was a big holiday for all Romans. They gave each other presents and held feasts. It was a time of happiness and good will.

The early Christian leaders thought it was a good idea to celebrate Christ's birthday at the time of such a happy festival. That is why we celebrate Christmas at the end of December.

Today the Temple of Saturn, in Rome, is in ruins.

The Yule log

The **Yule log** was cut down and dragged home to be burnt.

In northern countries, where winters are cold and dark, people used to burn giant logs of wood to keep themselves warm. The logs were called Yule logs, but nobody knows how they got that name.

Sometimes the Yule log was decorated with coloured ribbons. When it was burned, its ash was used as a good luck charm. The remains of the log were put in a box to keep the home safe from evil for the coming year.

People thought that evergreen trees brought good luck, too. So they decorated their homes with holly, ivy and mistletoe.

In the past, people cut mistletoe for their winter festival.

Eating and drinking

Christmas drinks

Since the time of the Roman Saturnalia, Christmas has been a time for eating and drinking.
The **wassail** bowl was a favourite in days gone by. 'Wassail' means 'good health'. The wassail bowl was very big and was filled with cider, brandy and spices. It was hung by a chain above the burning Yule log to heat up.

Father Christmas is holding the wassail bowl.

People acted in special Christmas plays, many years ago. This group of actors is entertaining a family at the door of their home. Everyone seems to be having a good time.

In castles and big houses the lord paid for the wassail. All the people living nearby had some of it. Sometimes people took the wassail bowl from house to house around the village. Everyone had a drink and then topped up the bowl with a drink of their own. It must have made a powerful mixture!

Farmers used to sell turkeys and geese at Christmas markets.

The main dish

Long ago, rich people ate many kinds of birds at Christmas – swans, geese, pheasants and peacocks.

Another favourite dish was roast boar's head. A boar is a kind of pig. The head was decorated with holly, and an apple, orange or lemon was stuck in its mouth.

Today many people eat roast turkey on Christmas Day. Turkeys came originally from North America. They were brought back to England by sailors. Since then, turkey has become a favourite Christmas dish.

Mince pies used to have minced meat inside them. They were oblong in shape to remind everyone of the **crib** in the stable in Bethlehem where Jesus was born. Some had a little pastry model of the baby Jesus on the top.

This roast boar's head is decorated with holly.

Other Christmas food

One of the best-known Christmas foods in the past was called 'frumenty'. It was like porridge, with nuts, eggs and honey added. Many people ate frumenty early on Christmas morning and again just before going to bed.

This Victorian cartoon shows how ill you can be if you eat too much Christmas pudding!

Christmas dinner has always been a favourite part of Christmas.

Another favourite Christmas food was called plum porridge. This was a thick soup made from meat, raisins and currants with spices and wine. The 'plum' part of it was dried plums or prunes.

Some people call Christmas pudding 'plum pudding', but today it has no plums or prunes in it at all. The pudding used to be steamed in a cloth, and was the shape and size of a football.

Fun and joy

Carol singing

Long ago there were special Christmas hymns that were sung in church. They had Latin words which most people could not understand.

Now we have Christmas carols which add fun and joy to Christmas.

At Christmas time, carol services are held in church.

At first, carols were songs that people danced to. Then new words were put to the tunes, telling the story of Christmas. Everyone was able to understand them. It was a good way of telling everybody about the baby Jesus.

Some carols are very old. The 'Holly and the Ivy', for example, tells of ideas that are older than Christianity. But nearly all today's best-known carols, such as 'O Come All Ye Faithful', 'Hark the Herald Angels Sing' and 'O Little Town of Bethlehem', were written not so long ago.

Good King Wenceslas

A vicar who lived in Victorian times found some very old tunes. He liked one of them very much and so wrote new words for it. This is the carol called 'Good King Wenceslas'. It tells how Wenceslas went out in the snow to give help to a poor man.

The real Wenceslas was a prince. He was the first person to tell the people of his land all about Jesus and Christianity.

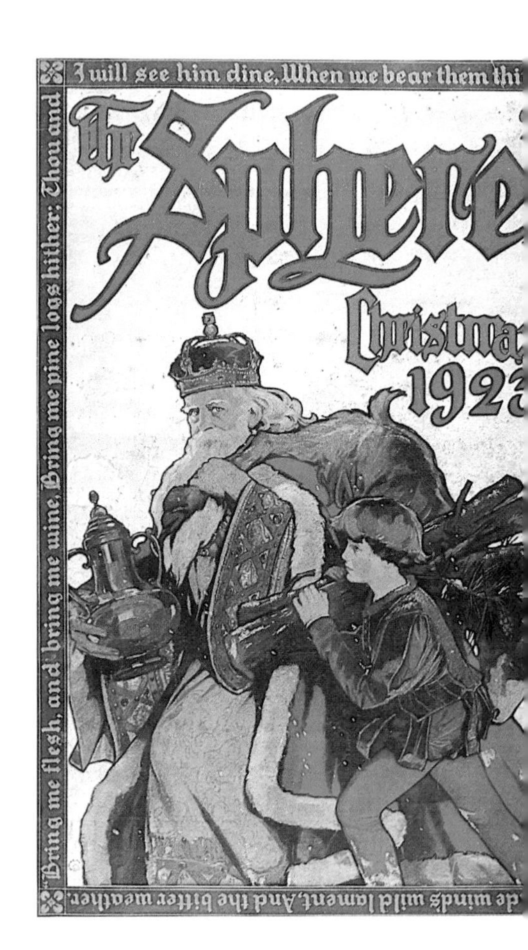

The musicians and singers who played and sang carols used to be called 'waits'. The waits in the picture on the opposite page seem to have forgotten that Christmas is a time of peace!

The Christmas crib

Another ancient part of Christmas is the **Christmas crib**. This is a model of the scene in the stable where Jesus was born.

Saint Francis, who lived in Italy long ago, first had the idea of making a crib. Only a small number of people could read and write in those days. Pictures in churches and on church windows told the Bible stories.

Saint Francis also loved all animals and birds.

The Christmas crib tells the story of Jesus' birth.

At Christmas time, Saint Francis decided to show people what the stable in Bethlehem looked like. He did not use models, as we do today. He used real people. Live animals, an ox and an ass, were also brought into this stable. The baby Jesus lying in his wooden crib was the only model. Saint Francis' idea spread. Today, cribs can be seen all over the world.

Christmas trees

The first Christmas trees probably came from Germany. Maybe trees were lit with candles to remind people of the starry sky over Bethlehem on the night Jesus was born.

The idea of Christmas trees spread from Germany to America and Britain. They were made popular in Britain by German-born Prince Albert, who was married to Queen Victoria. She was Queen from 1837–1901.

Some modern trees are huge. A famous one in the USA stands outside the White House. Another giant tree stands in Trafalgar Square in London.

Queen Victoria and her family enjoyed having a Christmas tree covered in presents.

This giant tree stands in a shopping centre in New York. ➧

Christmas cards and crackers

People gave each other gifts at Christmas as long ago as Roman times. But sending Christmas cards only began when Queen Victoria was alive.

It was probably a man called Sir Henry Cole who thought of the first Christmas card. His card, which you can see here, was decorated with vine leaves and showed people drinking. Today, a great many Christmas cards are sent every year.

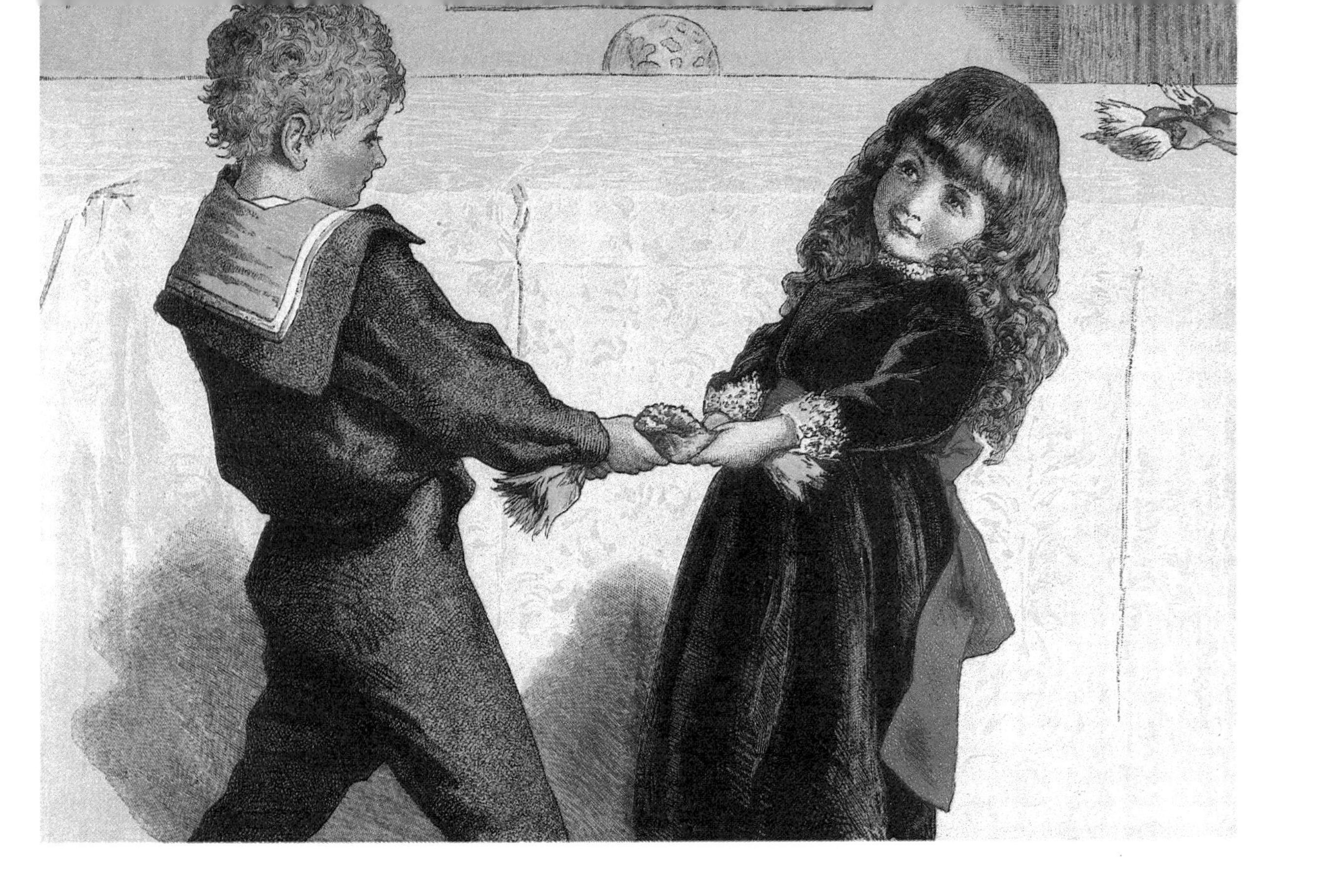

Christmas crackers were invented by a London pastry cook called Thomas Smith. On a visit to France he saw sweets wrapped up in paper with twisted ends. They gave him the idea for crackers. He also thought of putting in small toys, **mottoes** and bangers.

Who is Father Christmas?

Santa Claus

Today we think of Santa Claus and Father Christmas as the same person. In fact they are quite different.

The name 'Santa Claus' comes from the old Dutch word for Saint Nicholas. He was one of the first bishops of the Christian church.

Saint Nicholas is best remembered for his kindness to children. So he became the **patron saint** of children. His special day is close to Christmas. Over the years people came to believe that he gave presents to children.

This is an Australian Father Christmas. A small boy is telling him what he would like for his Christmas present.

People in stories

The idea of Father Christmas comes from the days long before Christianity. In those days people believed in many gods and goddesses. One god was called Odin.

People believed that Odin rode across the sky on a magic horse. At the end of December he gave gifts to those who had been good.

Father Christmas is usually shown with a long beard and wearing a red cloak. These ideas come from very old stories about a person with a red hood. Some stories say he was a dwarf, but others say he was tall with a cloak and a long white beard. In other stories he is dressed in green with a crown of holly.

Whatever he looks like, Father Christmas brings happiness at the darkest time of the year.

The Lord of Misrule

Many years ago, in the courts of kings and princes, someone was chosen at the start of Christmas to be the Lord of Misrule. He thought up games and jokes and funny plays. Everyone joined in the fun. This Lord of Misrule is wearing a pink and yellow costume.

Sometimes the Lord of Misrule took part in special Christmas plays. There would be a great deal of noise and merriment while the play was being performed.

Our modern idea of Father Christmas comes from all these people. Like Saint Nicholas, he brings presents for children. Odin's magic horse gives us the idea of the sleigh. Other old stories give us the white beard and red cloak. The Lord of Misrule added a sense of fun to Father Christmas.

These people are acting in a Christmas play about Saint George and the dragon.

The Christmas season

Advent

Advent is the time of year leading up to Christmas. People sometimes have a special Advent calender with windows. Inside each window there is a little picture. One window is opened each day, until Christmas Day. The last picture usually shows Jesus in the crib.

Pantomimes are special plays performed at Christmas time. They are lots of fun.

A special Christmas Eve game was called snapdragon. Raisins and brandy were put into a bowl and set alight. The players had to pick out a raisin from the flames. Snapdragon was played in the dark.

Boxing Day

Boxing Day, the day after Christmas, is the old feast day of Saint Stephen. He was supposed to look after horses. Because of this, sports with horses, such as hunting and racing, are often held on that day.

People also enjoyed hunting birds, such as wrens, and putting them in cages on Boxing Day. Today we think this is a cruel sport.

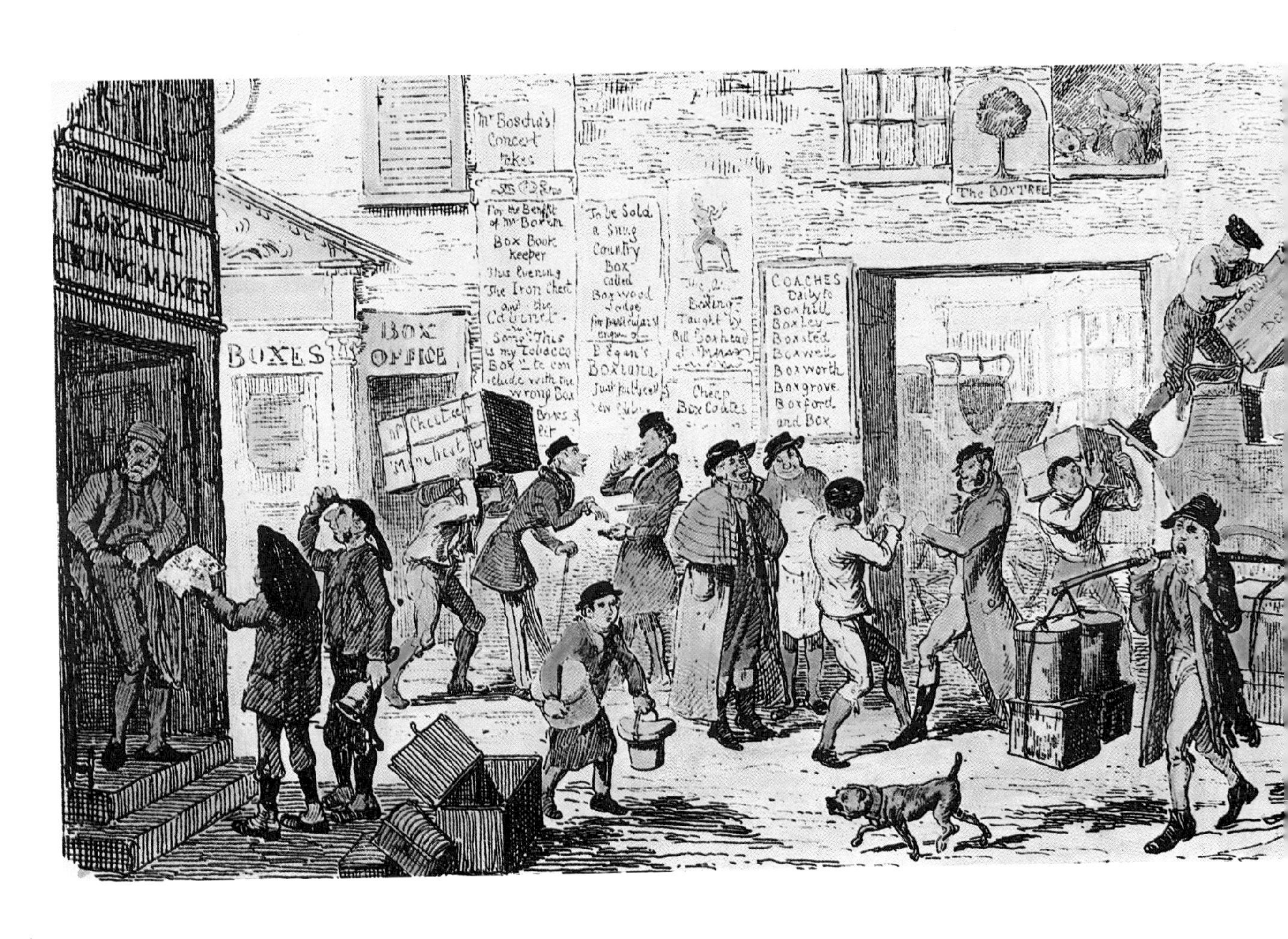

This is an old cartoon about Boxing Day. How many things in it can you see connected with the word 'box'?

How did Boxing Day get its name? It may be called after the boxes in churches at Christmas. People put money in the boxes to give to the poor. The boxes were opened the day after Christmas Day.

New Year's Eve

New Year's Eve is 31 December, the last day of the year. At midnight, bells ring out all over the world to welcome the New Year.

In Scotland, New Year is called **Hogmanay.** It is an even more important celebration than Christmas. In some towns a blazing tar barrel is carried through the streets. In this way the last of the old year is 'burned up' before the new one arrives.

Something else done in Scotland and the north of England at New Year is ‘first footing’. The first stranger to step into your house after midnight at New Year brings you good or bad luck. If it is a man with black hair carrying a small gift, it will bring you good luck.

This man is ‘first footing’ in Scotland.

Epiphany

Epiphany is on 6 January, the twelfth and last day of the Christmas season. It is the time when we celebrate the Three Wise Men visiting the baby Jesus in the stable. They brought him gifts of gold, frankincense and myrrh. Frankincense and myrrh are sweet-smelling oils.

The Three Wise Men followed the star to the place where Jesus was born.

Epiphany is also known as **Twelfth Night**. It is said to be bad luck to keep your Christmas decorations after that day, so people take them down. These children are burning theirs.

Twelfth Night used to be a time for special games and fun. Someone would be chosen as ‘king’, like the Lord of Misrule. Others then became his servants. They gave each other funny names and wore fancy dress.

Christmas around the world

In Mexico, children play a Christmas Day game with large jars of sweets. Each child is blindfolded and tries to break open one of the jars with a stick. The winner gets a prize and then the sweets are shared out.

This Christmas parade is in Australia.

In the southern half of the world, Christmas comes in midsummer. So, in Australia and New Zealand, people eat roast turkey and Christmas pudding, but they may have their dinner on a hot sandy beach.

Many countries celebrate Christmas even though they are not Christian countries. In the USSR, Father Christmas is known as Grandfather Frost. He brings presents to children. This Christmas display is in a shopping street in Japan.

Christmas in Bethlehem

Where Jesus was born

One of the most holy places at Christmas time is Bethlehem, which is where Jesus was born. It is now in Israel.

Many years ago a church was built in Bethlehem, called the Church of the **Nativity**. It is the oldest Christian church still in use anywhere in the world.

This is the cave of the Nativity, where people believe Jesus was born.

A special Christmas Eve service is held in the Church at Bethlehem.

Beneath the church is the cave of the Nativity, where people believe Jesus was born. On Christmas Eve many people visit the cave and then go into the small church for the service. Other people gather in the hills nearby at the place where the angels told the shepherds about the birth of Jesus.

Glossary

Advent The time from the beginning of December to Christmas Day.

Crib A wooden container for animal food. The new-born Jesus was placed in a crib. The **Christmas crib** is a model of the scene in the stable where Jesus was born.

Epiphany The 6 January, when we celebrate the Three Wise Men visiting the baby Jesus.

Hogmanay The Scottish name for New Year.

Mottoes Messages or jokes written on slips of paper and put inside crackers.

Nativity The birth of Jesus.

Patron saint A saint who looks after a special group of people.

Saturnalia A very old Roman festival which used to be held at the end of December. The Romans then remembered Saturn, their god of farming.

Twelfth Night The 6 January, the twelfth and last day of the Christmas season.

Wassail A spiced drink taken from a big bowl. 'Wassail' means 'good health'.

Yule log A big log of wood cut down and burned at Christmas time.

Books to read

Christmas by Lynne Armstrong (Macdonald, 1980)

The Lion Christmas Book by Mary Batchelor (Lion Publishing, 1986)

First Christmas by Lynne Bradbury (Ladybird books, 1984).

Christmas by Susannah Bradley (Macdonald, 1986)

First Christmas by Penny Frank (Lion Publishing, 1986)

First Christmas by Tomie de Paola (Metheun, 1984).

Christmas Book (Kingfisher Books, 1985)

Index

Acknowledgements

The publisher would like to thank all those who provided pictures on the following pages: BBC Hulton Picture Library 24; British Tourist Authority 39; D. Pike 44, N. O. Tomalin 5, 25 – Bruce Coleman Limited; Mary Evans Picture Library 6, 14, 15, 16, 17, 18, 20, 21, 22, 26, 27, 28, 32, 34, 37, 40, 41; Sonia Halliday Photographs 7; Alan Hutchinson Library 29; The Mansell Collection 8, 10, 12, 30, 33, 38; Peter Newark's Western Americana 11; Outlook Films Ltd. 19, 31; Ann & Bury Peerless 23; Picturepoint Ltd. 9, 35, 42, 43, 45; TOPHAM 4.